MW01089983

# BOOST YO

# MEDIA RESULTS

# REDUCE YOUR HOURS

## 200 FREE TOOLS TO SAVE TIME ON SOCIAL MEDIA MANAGEMENT

*I recommend not checking out all 200 tools at once as it's a lot of information and you will enjoy this book a lot more if you don't get overload.*

**Anita Nipane**

This book was written by Anita Nipane of Digginet.

Trademarks
All product and brand names mentioned in this book are used for their benefit with no intention toinfringe their copyrights. No such use is intended to convey endorsement or other affiliation with this book.

For more information, contact :
http://www.digginet.com

# DiggiNet

First Edition: October 2018

# YOUR FREE GIFT

Do you need to create images and simple banners for your webpage, blog, and social media?

The good news is – you don't need to hire a designer or buy expensive software to create visuals for the web. You can do it YOURSELF and with FREE tools. Thanks to the different resources that are available on the Internet. There are so many easy and quick solutions out there! Get my book "**100+ Free Tools to Create Visuals for Web & Social Media**" for FREE and learn how to:

- get royalty free images even for commercial purposes
- edit photos and create web banners with free online editors
- pick tasteful color combinations for your brand and web banners
- create simple animated gif banners
- take and edit screenshots as well as record tutorial videos from your screen
- remove the background from any image (no Photoshop or designer skills needed)
- add beautiful and free fonts to your computer

- create slideshows, presentations, and infographics

- "steal" color codes from any website

- use other tools that will save you time and improve your efficiency

**Available on www.digginet.com**

# Contents

# Do You Want to Spend Less Time Managing Social Media?

If you manage multiple social media profiles, then you know that to get results you need to create good quality content, post it regularly, create marketing campaigns, analyze their results, communicate with your followers, track hashtags, cooperate with influencers, spy on competitors... and the list goes on and on. Moreover, you need to do all this on a daily basis.

Even for a full-time social media manager, it may sound overwhelming, but if you are a small business owner, a blogger or an author who works on building his audience, it can be like a mission impossible. Because you also need to work on your daily business tasks. And you have your personal life, too.
So, do you feel like managing social media sucks up too much of your time?

You are not alone. One of the toughest challenges for many social media managers is creating content on a day-to-day basis. A Venngage infographic (https://venngage.com/blog/visual-content-marketing-statistics) shows that the number one struggle for 36.7% of marketers is **consistently** creating visual content.

Fortunately, you can save your time and make it more effortless if you do it in a smart way. Don't work for social media. Find a way to make social media work for you.

Every week, people build and launch new social media tools that can help us social media managers to be more productive and save time. I have listed 200 of them in this book.

Sounds overwhelming, doesn't it?

Don't worry. You don't need to use all of them. Simply go through the list, find the tools that will help you to be more productive, and implement your own unique social media management system. Not only will using these tools make your life a whole lot easier, they will also help you save money because most of them are free. This book will be your toolset that you can use as a manual every time you need to find a tool to automate your social media management tasks and become more productive. Actually, I'm using it as my manual, too and I'm happy to share it with you.

The tools I have listed in this book will help you manage multiple social media profiles in one place, schedule posts in advance, track analytics across platforms, create visuals, find influencers, spy on your competitors, get inspiration, track hashtags, create content calendar and the list goes on and on and on. They can really be game changers for your social media strategy. Buy this book and be one step ahead of your competitors!

## You Don't Need to Be Everywhere

But before we move on to the list of tools, let's decide which social media platforms you should be using. There are so many of them: Facebook, Instagram, Twitter, Snapchat, Periscope, YouTube, Vine, Google+, LinkedIn, Pinterest, Tumblr and few others that are emerging while I'm writing this book.

The good news is you don't have to be on all the social media platforms. Choose only the ones where your target audience hangs and make them work for you. Moreover, choose those platforms that feel the most effortless for you. Otherwise, it can easily become a sleeveless errand to try to be everywhere all at once. If you are not good at creating videos for YouTube, do not create a YouTube channel. Choose another social media platform instead. Sometimes it feels like you need to be everywhere, but it's not possible. Especially if you are a lone blogger or solopreneur. You can't be amazing on every social media platform. That takes a huge amount of time, effort and money. Choose one or two social media platforms instead and get the most out of them.

That being said, there are social media platforms that suit specific business models best, and if you belong to one of them, you should consider these particular social media platforms. For example, if you sell products that can be transformed into stunning photos like, visual arts, DIY or food, or you have a designer that can create something visually astonishing, spending your resources on Instagram and Pinterest would be a great idea. If you sell info products, like online courses and would like to have a connection with your audience on a more personal level, try YouTube videos. If you are going to share news updates and blog posts, Facebook and Twitter are a good choice. In any case, you should choose the platform that gives you the best return on investment.

There are many theories on how to set your social media marketing goals and create a strategy; however, I love the advice given by Guy Kawasaki in his book "The Art of Social Media":

"The gist of planning for social media and all content marketing is simple:
• Figure out how to make money.
• Figure out what kind of people you need to attract to make money.

• Figure out what those people want to read (which is probably different from what you want them to read)."

It's plain and simple. But now, let's move to the chapters about tools and resources you can use to save hours spent managing social media.

# Analyze Your Social Media Performance

There's no point in implementing a social media marketing plan if you don't track your results and evaluate the performance. There are many metrics you need to track: @mentions, shares, links, and impressions, audience growth rate, post reach, likes, favorites, engagement rate, click-through rate and cost, conversation rate and many others. Most of them you can see in the analytics section of each social media profile:

- Facebook - Audience Insights, Page Insights, and graph search
- Instagram – Instagram Insights
- Twitter – Twitter Analytics
- LinkedIn – LinkedIn Analytics
- Pinterest - Pinterest Analytics
- YouTube – YouTube Analytics

However, sometimes you need more data than the basic analytics every social media platform can provide. Moreover, it is much more convenient to see all your social media profile statistics in one place than to switch from one to another.

1. In this case, Metricool (http://www.metricool.com) can be handy. It will give you additional insights on your Facebook, Instagram, Twitter and LinkedIn profile statistics. The best part is that all the statistics are available in one place so that you don't need to navigate from one social media platform to another to get the full picture. It's free for one user.

2. A similar tool is Cyfe (http://www.cyfe.com). You can use it to monitor important metrics in one place. It allows you to customize your dashboard and set up widgets with different metrics of your social media profiles, email marketing, web performance and others. Cyfe allows you to create up to five widgets for free. If you need more than five, you will need to get their paid plan.

3. To get deeper insight on your Instagram profile performance, check out Union Metrics (https://unionmetrics.com/free-tools/instagram-account-checkup). Their free report will show you the best time to post to Instagram, what hashtags get you the most engagement, and what content performs best. You can also use their Twitter Assistant (https://unionmetrics.com/free-tools/twitter-assistant) to

get similar insights about your Twitter account performance.

4. Check out the free Instagram Analytics Tool (https://www.socialbakers.com/free-tools/tracker) made by Social Bakers to see your most popular and commented Instagram posts, distribution of posts by month, top performing color filters, and most tagged users.

5. Do you want to know your tweet indexation rate in Google Search? Then you will want to check out the Tweet Indexation Rate tool (https://congruentdigital.com/tweet-indexation-rate-tool). Simply enter your Twitter profile username and the tool will show you the Tweet indexation rate and the Page Authority of your profile.

6. Use Likealyzer (https://likealyzer.com) to evaluate your Facebook page performance. It will analyze your Facebook page data, your activity, likes growth, engagement rate and give you their Likerank (the higher, the better).

7. With the community members' report created by Sociograph (https://sociograph.io/landing.html), you can obtain valuable data about who the most active users in your Facebook community are. It can be very helpful if you want to contact them and build relationships so that they become your brand ambassadors. You can also get other

useful statistics and chance to compare it with that of your competitors.

8. If you manage a Facebook group, Grytics (https://grytics.com) can be helpful. It will give you statistics based on your most active members, engagement, and activity scores. Similarly, like Facebook page insights, Grytics gives you data on Facebook group posts. It's not free, though. The minimal price is 12 $ a month. However, if you are serious about growing your group, it might be worth it.

# Analyze Your Facebook Audience with Google Chrome Extensions

There are few "black hat" methods for analyzing your target audience and understanding your customer profile. Use one of the Google Chrome extensions that are listed below to find out personal information about your customers. This will help you understand who they are and what they are interested in, so you can prepare better offers for them.

1. Use Intelligence Search (https://www.intel-sw.com/blog/facebook-search) to find out, what Facebook groups the person has joined. It can be anyone. You don't have to be friends to be able to spy on this person. You can also find all Facebook posts that this person has liked.

Or, you can get a list of all persons that are interested in a particular topic and have joined the related groups. This can be helpful if you want to build relationships with them or invite them to join your own Facebook group. Just don't get spammy. Simply browse through the profiles to understand their interests and lifestyle. There are many more features you can use to find useful information on Facebook. So, check out this tool.

2. If you want to know about all activities that a person has made on Facebook, for example, the pages he likes, the places he has visited, photos commented, videos posted, groups joined and 20 more activities, use a Google Chrome Extension - Secret Revealer (http://www.andreamillozzi.it/addon/secretrevealerfb).

Download the extension, then open the Facebook profile you want to analyze, open the Secret Revealer and click "Search". You will be impressed by the information you can find on Facebook about anybody. I hope, you won't use this for stalking people, though. But it can help to write personalized messages to persons you want to relate with.

3. A similar tool is Social Media Advanced Search (https://bit.ly/2EUTs0i). Check out both tools and decide which works better for you.

4. A useful tool for Facebook automation is a Google Chrome extension, Toolkit for Facebook (https://www.toolkit-for-fb.com). It helps to perform actions in bulk, for example, you can invite all your friends to like your page, attend an event or join a group. You can also use this tool to click all "Add friend" buttons on a page. However, be careful with this not to get banned.

# Automate Reporting

If you need to create a report about social media marketing or web page performance, DataStudio.Google.com can save you a lot of time. It allows you to create visual dashboards easily for yourself, your boss or a customer. Log into Google Data Studio with your Google account and connect other sources of data like Facebook Ads Manager or Google Analytics. Google will import your data to the Data Studio, so that you don't need to spend time copying and pasting them. Create whatever kind of dashboard you want. Then drag and drop elements such as bar charts, pie charts, tables and others, add elements and your metrics. When you're done, you can easily share the report with your team members.

However, there is even an easier way to create social media reports fast. Octoboard (https://www.octoboard.com/business) will collect all your data from different resources (Facebook, Twitter, YouTube, Google Analytics, MailChimp and many other apps) in one place and visualize them in reports. Therefore, you will save a lot of time on collecting and analyzing data. Moreover, it will take much less time on being up-to-date on your social media marketing performance. With Octoboard free account, you can create 2 dashboards with 10 widgets. The paid plans start from 5$/month.

# Spy on Your Competitors

You and your competitors are after the same audience. This is a good reason to know what they are doing. You do not have to be a rocket scientist or growth hacker to spy on your competitors on social media.

Either you have a retail site, or a blog, the following tools and tips can be very helpful in getting to know more about your competitor followers, the content they share and their engagement rate. This will help you to understand on which social media platforms your audience may be most active.

# Facebook

The simplest and easiest way to benchmark your and your competitor Facebook profiles is to use "Pages to Watch" feature in Your Facebook page "Insights" section (Your Facebook page needs to have at least 100 fans for you to be able to create a list of Pages to watch). This feature allows you to watch other Facebook pages so you can compare their number of followers and audience growth, posting frequency and engagement rates to your own. This feature is handy if you want to see how well similar niche Facebook pages are performing. You can monitor any page you want on Facebook. You don't even have to follow it.

However, if you want to be up- to- date with your competitor's activities on Facebook, follow their Facebook page. Then choose "**See first**" to see all their posts in your newsfeed. You can even set notifications to see all notifications from this Page (up to 5 per day). This way, you will always be aware of what content your competitors are posting.

There are also various ways that make it very easy to see what ads your competitors are running and who they are targeting. Having this information will help you to create more successful promotions and better-targeted ads.

Visit your competitor's webpage and browse through specific sections or products to see if your competitor uses Facebook retargeting ads. If they do, you will be included in their *Website Custom Audience* list and will start seeing more and more bottom of the funnel ads from your competitor on your Facebook newsfeed. They'll be sending their latest ads right to you, so you will not need to search for them.

Next, when you see your competitor's ad or a sponsored post on Facebook, click the down-arrow on the top right corner and you will see "Why am I seeing this?"

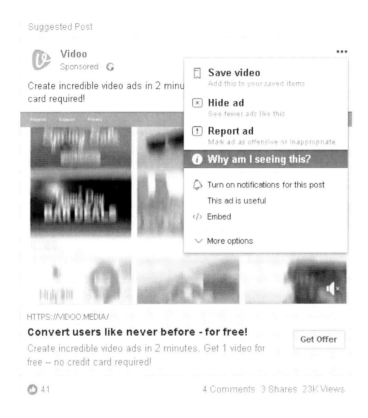

Click on it and Facebook will tell you what targeting your competitor is doing.

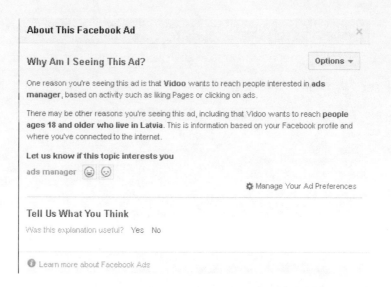

In this case, I was seeing the ad because Facebook had included me in their "ads manager" interest group. So, if I wanted to run a similar Facebook ad, it would be a good idea to target people that are interested in "ads manager". You can also click on the "This ad is useful" button to let Facebook know that you want to see more ads from this company on your newsfeed.

Recently Facebook released a new and completely free tool that is accessible for everyone. It is called **Info and Ads**. Visit any Facebook page you are interested in and check out the active ads that it is running. This tool allows you to spy with a click of a button. Moreover, you can use geographical filters to check in what locations your competitor runs their ads.

In case you want to see more Facebook ads, use the tool Ad Espresso (https://adespresso.com/ads-examples). It is a free tool that provides a huge database of published Facebook Ads. Use this tool to spy on your competitors' content strategy and get inspiration.

A similar tool is AdFox (http://www.adfox.io). It will show you Facebook ads and sales funnels in a matter of seconds. It offers 3-day free trial. Afterward, the cost is $39 – $67/month.

Use the online tool Fanpage Karma (http://www.fanpagekarma.com) to analyze your and your competitor account performance on Facebook. You'll be able to compare the page performance index, number of followers, average weekly growth and engagement rate. Get their Google Chrome extension to do your competitor evaluation while browsing through the Facebook business pages you are interested in. If you want to see the comparison across other social media platforms too, you will need to get Fanpage Karma paid plan.

Spy on your competitors and use the information obtained to create more engaging posts and get new target audiences. After doing this small research, you'll understand what your competitor thinks their strong points are. Moreover, you'll be able to find weak points in their ad strategies and win with better targeting or a stronger sales pitch. However, Facebook is just a part of a larger marketing strategy. Look at the rest of your competitor's marketing activities to get a deeper understanding what other marketing tools and techniques they use.

## Twitter

It's amazing what data you can find out about any profile that actively uses Twitter marketing. You can literary spy on them. All you need to do is search for their profiles and analyze their marketing tactics and techniques by doing reverse engineering. Look at their tweets and analyze what and how often they tweet, what is the goal of your competitor tweets – do they use Twitter to generate traffic to their website, build their email list, promote sales campaigns, build brand and their followers' loyalty? What Twitter marketing tactics do they use? If they constantly use the same techniques over a long period, most probably these tactics work for them.

There are also several tools you can use free of charge to analyze your competitor Twitter profiles and their performance. All these tools also have paid features that you can use for deeper analysis if you wish, but you can also get rather good insights by using only their free features.

1. If you want to find out who has higher Twitter profile ranking – you or your competitors, use Followerwonk (https://moz.com/followerwonk/compa

re) or try Social Blade (https://socialblade.com) Twitter profiles comparison report. You will see the percentage of retweets as well as future predictions. Additionally, use Twitter Analytics Report Card (https://bit.ly/2xo2ehO) to measure the quality of your content against your competition.

2. One of the best free tools for analyzing your and your competitor's Twitter profile is Twitonomy (https://www.twitonomy.com). You can get loads of useful information from this free tool. Simply sign in with your Twitter profile and you will see how often and what times your competitors post their tweets, their mentions, likes and retweets statistics, public lists the profiles are included and other data. It's a good tool also if you want to search within your own Twitter followers to find your potential cooperation partners or customers. Check out my YouTube video (https://youtu.be/qtzUp9xTrsM) to learn how to use Twitonomy for this purpose.

3. Foller (https://foller.me) is a quick tool that will show you general Twitter profile information, the main topics your competitor talks about, and their most popular hashtags, as well as mentions and analysis for the last 100 tweets. Of

course, you can use this tool for analyzing your own profile, too.

4. To monitor all your competitor tweets in one place, create a secret Twitter list (https://help.twitter.com/en/using-twitter/twitter-lists). Click on your profile photo to see the menu and choose "Lists." Create a new list and make it private (only visible to you) so that your competitors don't know you are spying them.

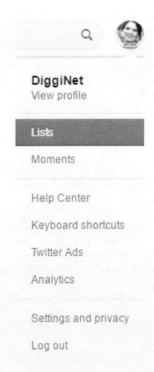

Then add to this list all profiles you want to monitor. Just go to the profile you want to include in your list and open the menu by clicking on the three dots near "Follow" button. Then choose "Add or remove from lists." Now you will always be up-to-date regarding your competitor activities on Twitter.

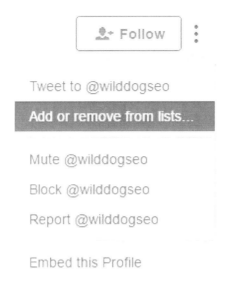

5. If you want to find out the engagement rate for every tweet of your chosen account – either competitor's or yours, check out SocialBearing (https://socialbearing.com). You will see how many tweets a day your competitors post, in how many lists the account is added and other interesting data. The results may surprise you. Just write

down the handle of the Twitter account you want to spy on and see the results.

6. Use Twitter Advanced Search (https://twitter.com/search-advanced) tool to know what conversations your competitors are having on Twitter. Simply search for the @username of your competitor. You can also specify the period, and location, hashtags, keywords and other parameters to narrow down the results. Save this search by clicking on the more icon (three dots) at the top of your results page to quickly use it whenever you need it. Next time you click the search box, a pop-up menu will display your saved searches.

Therefore, you can see the newest mentions of your competitors. You can create similar searches for mentions of your profile or any other Twitter profile you are interested in, as well.

If you want to track tweets from certain people or companies, subscribe to get SMS notifications on your mobile phone each time they tweet a new post. This way, you won't miss them. For example, if you want to monitor all tweets Madonna posts, follow her and set up a tweet alert on her account like in the picture below so that you won't miss any post.

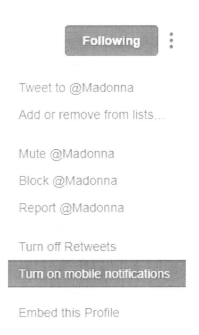

If you would like to learn how to automate your Twitter marketing and other Twitter marketing hacks, get my book "**Automate Your Twitter Marketing: Build Your Brand, Get New Followers and Drive Traffic to Your Website**".

# YouTube

If you want to do competitive research to find out which are the dominant YouTube channels in your industry, use Socialbakers' free monthly benchmark reports (https://www.socialbakers.com/statistics/youtube/channels).

Choose which platform you would like to analyze (in this case, YouTube), the country you are targeting, and your niche to reveal the top influencers. The categories here are rather broad, so you will need to find the brands that are most similar to your own. Explore their channels to see what type of videos is drawing the greatest engagement and views.

You can be more specific and compare several channel statistics to find out how your YouTube channel compares to others.
Use Social Blade comparison tool (https://socialblade.com/youtube/compare) to see your competitors subscriber rank, video views, estimated earning potential, future predictions and other data.

Go even deeper by using TubeBuddy (https://www.tubebuddy.com) or VidIQ (https://vidiq.com) to see analytics of every YouTube video you are watching. You will see not only statistics like channel total views, social media engagement rate and average daily subscriber growth, but also tags or keywords used for this video. Many YouTubers do not know how to use tags correctly, although they are one of the most important techniques to get your videos ranked on YouTube. However, thanks to these tools, you will be able to copy your competitor tags and use them for your own videos if they are on a similar topic. Both tools have free plans for beginners and offer different functionality that complements each other; therefore, it's best to use them simultaneously. VidIQ offers in-depth analytics of other people videos; it will allow you to benchmark your competitors and provide other functionality for free. But TubeBuddy will show you keyword score so you know which keywords to optimize your videos for. It will also provide video topic planner functionality and will show and copy video tags, so you can optimize your video keywords for SEO. For best functionality, download Google Chrome extensions of both tools – TubeBuddy and VidIQ.

# Pinterest

The first and the simplest way to find out what's popular with your competitor's audience is to visit their Pinterest pages. Check out what types of topics are popular among their audiences and what their pinning strategy is. All you need to do is go to your competitors' profiles and click on their Activity tab. Here you will see the pins that have been saved by their audience.

To dig even deeper into the minds of your competitor's audience, try searching the web page address, for example, competitor.com in the Pinterest search box to see pins from your competitor's website. This way, you will know what content your audience is interested in.

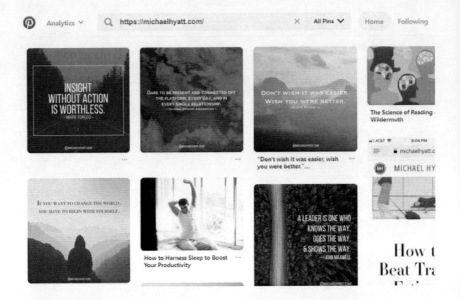

Unfortunately, there are not so many free tools for analyzing Pinterest accounts. However, if you use the pro version of Tailwind (https://www.tailwindapp.com), you can keep track of your Pinterest competitors and how they are doing, including their engagement rates.

# Who are Influencers?

Being friends with influencers is important. If somebody who has hundreds of thousands of followers shares your content or sends an email about your new product to their million email subscribers, you can get rich and famous in minutes. However, most often it doesn't happen like this. Influencers, like Neil Patel, Michael Hyatt, Oprah Winfrey and others are huge business owners who receive hundreds of emails every day. They have their own interests and cooperation partners who are equally influential. Unless you have something truly unique to share, it's almost impossible to get noticed by them. But still, you can benefit from the idea of being friends with influencers.

Who actually are influencers? They are people who have the power to influence the perception of others to get them to change their behavior or decisions. Or, in simple words thanks to their recommendations, people would buy from you. There is a misconception that influencers must have a huge social media following. It's not true and confuses influence with popularity.

Of course, it's great if your influencer has a huge following, but he can also have only few hundreds of followers or less. But imagine, if all these followers are very loyal to him and have trust in his recommendations? Those influencers with high credibility and good salesmanship are called micro-influencers. Every industry has thought-leaders to whom people look for inspiration and advice. You just need to find them.

Therefore, when considering marketing strategy for your new product launch or sales promotion, you need to decide first if you are going to target influencers with a huge following or micro-influencers, or both. Your decision would mainly depend on your own influence and market power. If you are an influencer with a huge following, then it will be rather easy to contact other influencers with a huge number of followers. Because you can offer them a barter, for example, to send information about their promotion to your followers, when they need it. If you have a small or non-existing following, then it will be easier to contact micro-influencers, because you have nothing to offer except useful information or product.

Of course, one more option is to pay money to influencers. Advertisers have used celebrities in their campaigns for decades. You, too, can pay money to influencer. Or, you can build sincere personal relationships to get them want to help you for free.

Influencers want to be recognized and be the first who have access to new and useful information because they need it to strengthen their influence. If you have an interesting and useful product, it should be easy to arise their interest.

**There are two ways to evaluate your influencers:**

1. Context: Does this person fit with your brand? The influencer must have an audience that is interested in your product. For example, if you want to promote your cookbook, then you need to find an influencer whose audience is interested in cooking. Most probably, it would be a chef or recipes blogger.

2. Reach: Does this person have a good following with a high engagement rate? There is no use of million followers if there is zero engagement rate. Therefore, before choosing your influencers, evaluate both criteria.

## Identifying Influencers through Social Media

There are many social media marketing platforms that help brands find the best influencers for their niche and vice versa. These platforms usually collate a database of people they believe are influential on social media and/or through blogging. They can function as invitation only when influencers must apply for being a part of the platform or completely automated systems. In both cases, these platforms usually have powerful analytics and search engines.

1. Take a look at one of the world's largest influencer discovery and directory tools - HyprBrands (https://hyprbrands.com). You can find over 10 million influencers globally here and will get access to detailed audience demographics. The platform shows information about all social media accounts the influencer owns. You can create a list of the preferred influencers and export it as a pdf file.

2. A similar tool is Scrunch (https://scrunch.com). It also provides a huge list of influencers in different categories and on different social media platforms. Use free trials of both tools to explore their features.

3. If you want to find influencers who write about particular topics, use Brand24 (https://brand24.com). Although the main purpose of this tool is to help you discover what people are saying online about your brand, you can also use it to find influencers. Search for social media or blog posts using your keywords and you will get a list of latest publications that have influencer scores assigned to them. Use influencer filter (based on a scale 0–10) to quickly get to the most relevant posts. The last step is to identify those who you consider worth cooperating with and contact them.

4. Categorize influencers by their types: bloggers, journalists, companies and others with BuzzSumo (https://app.buzzsumo.com). Although their free plan is rather limited, still, you can make use of it in three valuable ways.

- First, you can find the most shared content about the topic you are interested in and see who shared it.

- Second, you can find influencers based on keywords and hashtags.

- And last, it is possible to filter influencers based on types, such as companies, bloggers and journalists.

All these features are available in one simple dashboard. Therefore, you can do a quick analysis to reveal the most successful type of content in your niche, and who to contact to spread it.

5.  Score influencer profiles with Kred (https://home.kred). This tool measures social influence by providing two scores, called "Influence" and "Outreach". "Influence" measures the likelihood that someone will engage with the user's posts, and "Outreach" measures the user's tendency to share content created by others. These scores can help you identify the most influential Twitter users that could be willing to share your content.

6.  If you are looking for YouTube influencers who would be interested in getting hired by a brand, check out Famebit (https://famebit.com). It is a YouTube-focused influencer network.

7.  Use Twitonomy (http://www.twitonomy.com) to find influencers among your Twitter followers. Search for keywords within Twitter user bios and sort their profiles by largest number of followers. Open their profiles and check out their tweets analytics, most popular tweets, mentions and other data that will help you to take the right decision.

In the result, you will have a list of followers to target as prospective cooperation partners.

8. You can find influencers while using your email, too. Discover.ly (http://discover.ly) is a Google Chrome extension for Gmail that you can use to find social media influencers among your cooperation partners, customers and other people who send you emails. These plugins will display social connection information about your contacts. In simple words, it means that you will be able to see the social profiles of persons that are writing you emails. Right in your inbox. Give it a shot. It's really useful.

Facebook is also working on a new tool – Facebook Brand Collabs manager (https://www.facebook.com/collabsmanager/start) that will help connect marketers to social media influencers. It will show how closely a creator's audience matches yours based on criteria like interests, gender, age range and more. Unfortunately, this tool is currently available to limited brands and creators focusing on the U.S. market. However, it might change in the future. If you're interested in gaining access, you will need to subscribe to their waitlist.

If you are serious about doing influencer marketing, check out this list of platforms (https://www.stedavies.com/influencer-marketing-platforms) that curate thousands of influencer profiles you can choose from. You will not only be able find the best influencers but also analyze the performance of your influencer marketing campaigns to see which influencers gave you the best results.

## Track Hashtags & Keywords

Hashtags are a great way to get additional exposure to your posts, reach new audiences and attract new followers. Since hashtags work as keywords when somebody searches for a specific content, they help non-followers to find your posts. And if they like your content, they may decide to hit the follow button. Therefore, identifying the best performing and most relevant hashtags for each of your social media posts is very important.

Additionally, if you are promoting a new product or launching a contest, a branded hashtag can help you track the results of your campaign. Thanks to the branded hashtag, you will see all interactions and all posts that include your hashtag. Moreover, you can monitor the performance of hashtags with hashtag analytics tools.

So, check out the list below to choose the best tool for your purpose.

## Twitter

1. A cool tool for automating and analyzing your hashtags is Ritetag (https://ritetag.com). It provides automatic hashtag suggestions if you upload your image or write text in their tool. The hashtags are color-graded based on real-time engagement. Therefore, you can see which hashtags are popular at the time you are creating your post. Ritetag will auto-hashtag your posts with hashtags that are both relevant and currently trending. It will also save your time by automatically @mentioning the author of an article whose post you are sharing and replacing words with emoji or hashtags. Check out also their other functionality with the free trial. For additional functionality, use Ritetag Chrome/Firefox/Safari extension and Android app.

2. Find out which are the most retweeted tweets and biggest contributors of your competitors by using TweetReach (https://tweetreach.com) and Tweetbinder (http://www.tweetbinder.com). You can also analyze estimated reach and top contributors of specific hashtags.

3. One more tool you can use is Hashtagify (http://hashtagify.me). It will show you the latest trending hashtags related to the topics you are interested in. Just write your keyword in their search engine and see the

related hashtags as well as their popularity index. You can get this functionality free of charge. Make your own hashtag list and use them when necessary. Read more about using hashtags in my article "How to Get the Most Out of Twitter Hashtags?"on www.digginet.com.

4. If you need to find out what a particular hashtag is being used for, you will want to check out Twubs (http://twubs.com). It's a hashtag directory that you can use to research and shortlist hashtags that you should be following and using. Moreover, you can register your own branded hashtag to control its feed, because Twubs will provide you with a branded landing page (paid option). It means that you will be able to block users and negative word usage as well as remove negative posts. And in case it's necessary, you will have a record that can be used in any legal challenge.

5. Keyhole (http://keyhole.co) is a paid service but it offers a free preview of its features. You can use it to track hashtags on Twitter and Instagram. Their free preview will show you the number of users who have posted with your tracked hashtag, engagements, related topics, top posts and other data.

## Instagram

1. Upload your image to Instagram hashtag generator (https://influencermarketinghub.com/instagram-hashtag-generator) and it will suggest you a list of hashtags that you can use for this image. Since hashtags are sorted by popularity, you can choose those that are trending. If you feel like you need more ideas, choose up to five keywords to generate the most popular associated hashtags. Then select all hashtags you would like to copy by marking the checkboxes and press "Copy Selected Hashtags". And paste them in your Instagram post. That's all.

2. Pixlee (https://www.pixlee.com/analytics-dashboard/reports) will provide you a free weekly report with hashtag statistics, growth in Instagram followers, and most engaging posts. It will help you identify social media influencers and find brand advocates posting about your brand. Use this information to connect with social influencers and brand advocates.

3. Use Leetags (https://leetags.com) app to save your time on choosing hashtags for your Instagram posts. Simply write your keyword and this app will provide you a list of most relevant hashtags related to your subject. A cool feature is that the app auto-selects the top 30 hashtags

that you can copy right away. Or, you can select and copy only those hashtags that you want. Then save the results of your searches or add your chosen hashtags to favorites. Therefore, next time when you need these hashtags, you will be able to copy and paste them quickly.

4. If you are an iPhone user, you may want to try the app Command (https://commandforig.com). It will help you understand your Instagram account performance better by providing post analytics. You will see the best time to post and will get personalized hashtag recommendations. This app is also great for seeing which of the people you follow are following you back.

## Instagram

Similarly, like with any other social media platform, you can also spy on your Instagram competitors by following them. If you visit your competitors' profiles and engage with their content often, Instagram will show their posts on your newsfeed. But if you want to be sure that you ALWAYS see their posts on your newsfeed, click the three dots in the right upper corner of the Instagram post and turn on post notifications.

In case your competitor has a branded hashtag, follow it too. This way, you will always be up to date with what is being posted. Simply find it and then press "Follow" button.

1. It's easy to benchmark followers count and see who has more followers – you or your competitor, but engagement is a much more important metric. Use a free Instagram engagement calculator Phlanx (https://phlanx.com) to find out what engagement rate you and your competitors have. You can also benchmark several Instagram profiles to see who performs the best.

2. There are tools that will help you to get a deeper analysis on your competitor performance, for example, use free plan of the app Metricool (https://app.metricool.com) to monitor up to five Instagram competitors. You will see the average number of likes, comments, interaction number by the date, and the latest posts.

3. A similar tool is Social Insider (https://www.socialinsider.io). You can use either one of their paid plans or check out their functionality by using trial version. Additionally, to general statistics like, fan growth and engagement rate of your competitors, you will

also see their most popular hashtags, most engaging posts, what post types they use (image, video, carousel) and what time your competitors usually post.

4.  Analyze your or any other Instagram account for fake followers with this simple tool (https://bit.ly/2EOZiA4) created by Influencer Marketing Hub. You will find out the estimated audience quality score, engagement rate and likes-comment ratio. Or, if you want a deeper analysis, try Deep Social (https://deep.social). It will estimate what percentage of engagement comes from influencers, the audience demographics, location by country, influencer relevant keyword cloud, popular hashtags, mentions and other interesting data.

5.  Create a free Squarelovin (https://www.squarelovin.com) account and get access to metrics on your recent Instagram posts and growth, a monthly analysis, and a history of your posts broken down into year, month, day, and hour. Get more insights on your communities' preferences and interests, and what drives engagement. Squarelovin even shows you your best and worst times to post.

# Create a Content Calendar

A content calendar helps you plan out the content that you intend to publish on your blog and social media accounts. It also helps plan your posting sequence. For example, if you write a blog, you can plan to write several blog posts and then schedule these posts to be published over several weeks using one of the post scheduling tools that you will find in the next chapter. Your content calendar should include all social media activities that you will do to promote your content, organized by date and time. Make sure that your content supports your business goals.

Your content calendar should include the following information: title or short description of the content, links to resources for creating the content, its author, deadline and channels you are going to use for promotion (web page, social media, e-mails, cooperation partners, etc.).

There are several theories about what type of content should be published and in what proportions. One of them is that you need to follow the rule of thirds:

- One-third of your social media content is educational, entertaining and informative and is either created by your company or by influencers in your industry
- One-third of your social media content is personal interactions with your audience (surveys, questions, comments, answers to their questions)
- One-third promotes your business and sales offers

Or, you can follow the 80-20 rule which is easier for beginners and solopreneurs who are starting from scratch. In this case, 80% of your posts should be informative, educational, inspirational and entertaining, but 20% should - promote your business, discounts and other sales promotions.

Planning these different post types in your content calendar will help you maintain the correct ratio. A good rule of thumb is that about 50% of your content should include links to drive traffic to your blog.

Now, let's look at the tools you can use for creating your content calendar.

1. Actually, you don't need a specific tool. You can use a tool that you might be already familiar with. It's Google Calendar (https://calendar.google.com/calendar). You can create a separate calendar within your regular calendar and devote it for planning your content. If there are several persons that work on your social media content, invite them as your team members. Additionally, you can use different colors for different content and add reminders. It's really easy to use, free of charge and is accessible online from every device.

2. You can also use Google Spreadsheets (https://www.google.com/sheets/about). Write a list of your planned social media posts with the posting dates and assign tasks to your team members to later track the status. Don't forget to share the file with your team members to give them rights to edit and update the information. Or, give them rights only to comment or view the file.

3. If you prefer using MS Office products, get the same functionality from MS One Drive. You will get the same functionality as from Google Drive, but will work in Excel file that can be easily opened offline directly in Excel on your computer.

4. Trello (https://trello.com) is another tool that's great for team collaboration. You can use it to map out to-do lists, manage your content calendar and for other purposes.

5. If you love using Evernote, you can create your Social media content calendar there, too. Simply download one of their calendar templates (https://bit.ly/2kFSEms) and start using it.

6. Or, use a ready-to-use content calendar developed by Airtable (https://airtable.com). Plan your content, post attachments, notes, links and add collaborators. Use their free plan or upgrade for a reasonable price to their premium plan.

There are many other tools you can use for creating your content calendar. If you feel that you need something more advanced than the free solutions I listed before, check out this list of 12 best social media calendars: https://bit.ly/2XnJpch.

## Content Creation

If you want to be successful on social media, you need to constantly create new content, which is a time-consuming process. Therefore, it is good to know how to do it in a productive and time efficient way.

**There are three categories of social media content:**

1. Original content - it is content that has been created by you or your team (articles, visuals, videos, SlideShare presentations and any other type of content.

2. Repurposed content – it is your original content that you can transform in other forms, for example, repack your blog posts into a new eBook, turn them into SlideShare presentations or other forms of content.

3. Curated content – a content that is created by other authors that you willingly share on your social media accounts because it's valuable for your audience and you are building relationships with the content authors.

Now, let's look at each of these content categories closer to see how you can spend less time creating it.

## Original Content – What is Trending?

Usually, one of the most difficult parts of creating a new content is finding ideas. There are so many options available. How to choose the right one?

First, you need to know what others have published about your topic and if there is a demand for this type of content. Do people engage with it?

1. One of the easiest and unfortunately most expensive ways to find it out is using BuzzSumo (https://buzzsumo.com). It will show you the top content with your chosen keywords that has been shared the most across multiple social media platforms.

2. A similar tool is Brand24 (https://brand24.com). I already told you about both tools in the chapter about finding influencers. Depending on your budget, you can use either their free or paid functionality.

3. One more option is Ahrefs (https://ahrefs.com/content-explorer). It is an expensive tool that will help you discover the most popular content for any topic (by backlinks, organic traffic and social shares). The good news is that

you can get its 7-day trial for 7$. In some cases, it might be enough to get insight in your niche.

4. One more way to find popular topics is using Google AdWords tool Keyword Planner (https://ads.google.com/home/tools/keyword-planner). You will need to create AdWords account to use this tool. Simply write your keywords in its search engine and find out the number of monthly searches on Google. The higher the number, the higher the demand is for the particular topic.

5. Additionally, you can use a plugin Keywords Everywhere (https://keywordseverywhere.com/google-search-volume.html) that will instantly show you the search volume for every keyword and its cost per click (in case you want to use it for an AdWords campaign) while you are browsing on the Internet. So, you won't need to use Keyword Planner. Currently, it supports the following platforms: Google Search, YouTube, Bing, Amazon, eBay, and others. It means that every time you write a keyword in their search box, you'll see the keyword's monthly search volume.

6. Combine Keywords Everywhere with Soolve (https://soovle.com) to get the most of both tools. Enter

your keywords in Soolve search engine to see what your audience is searching for on different Internet platforms like, Yahoo, Bing, Amazon, YouTube, Wikipedia and Answers.com. You will get a list of many long tail keywords. They are more specific keyword phrases that visitors use when they're searching for information on the Internet.

7. To find hot and recent articles, use Google Search. Write your keywords in Google search engine, then choose the "News" tab and in the "Tools" section choose the period, for example, the current week. Therefore, you can find newest articles in your niche, assess their popularity and write a relevant article with your opinion on the topic. You can also receive Google alerts (https://www.google.com/alerts) about the topics you are interested in and be up to date on the news in your industry.

8. A cool tool for finding hot topics for your blog post is Answer the Public (https://answerthepublic.com). Write your keywords in its search box and the tool will provide you with a list of questions that your audience is interested in regarding the topic. The results are based on Google and Bing searches and, for example, questions

posted on Quora and similar platforms. Therefore, you will get a hint of the motivations and emotions of the people you are going to write for. Moreover, you can click on every suggested question to see the Google search behind it and visualize the data. But, in the bottom of the page, you will see a list of keywords that you can download as a csv (Excel) file and use to optimize your article for search engines.

9. Use Quora (https://www.quora.com) to find the most often asked questions in your niche. By searching the topic your content focuses on, you'll be able to find what questions people are asking. Write articles to answer them. This will help you to create a good quality content that addresses your audience needs. Besides, you can publish answers to the questions on Quora and direct readers to your blog posts for deeper insights. This strategy will help you to gain additional exposure and traffic to your website.

# Generate Viral Titles

There are two approaches you can use to decide on the topic for your blog post. First, you decide on the topic and then write its title. Second, you choose the title first and then write your article. In case you feel more comfortable with the second approach or need help to decide your title, you will want to check out these tools.

1. Use Blog About (https://www.impactbnd.com/blog-title-generator/blogabout) to get inspiration for your title. The tool will suggest different title structures that you can complement with your keywords. Add the titles you liked to your list and then send them to your email so that you can use them later.

2. Or, get a list of auto-generated titles with The Hoth Headline Generator (https://www.thehoth.com/headline-generator). You will need to enter your keywords and the tool will give you a list of ideas.

3. Similar tools are Tweak Your Biz Title Generator (https://tweakyourbiz.com/title-generator), Awesome Titles (http://www.title-generator.com), and FatJoe (https://fatjoe.co/blog-title-generator). Check them out,

generate titles for your content and include them in your content calendar.

# 9 Image Editing Online Tools You Should Know About

Most probably you know that social media and blog posts with pictures usually bring much better results than simple texts without any visual material or poorly designed and bad looking images. Therefore, it is important to create good quality images that attract your target audience. The good news is that these days you don't need a lot of money or professional design service to create a visual for your website or social media. Actually, it is a feasible task for every Internet or smartphone user, and it can be done almost or completely for free using online image editors. You don't even need to install any specific software.

All you need is using one of these image-editing tools that can be found online:

1.  One of such tools is PicMonkey (http://www.picmonkey.com). It offers many quality image creating and processing functions – backgrounds, borders, effects, symbols, photo processing possibilities, etc. One of the main advantages of this tool is the eye-catching font selection. These can be used for attracting attention and highlighting the most important parts of the text. In order to use your fonts (including Cyrillic or

Russian fonts and fonts with special characters or language fonts that are housed on your computer), go to "Add Text" – "Yours." If you want to learn how to add new fancy and free fonts to your computer to use them on your own software or in online image editing tools, watch this video tutorial: (https://youtu.be/5h4T5spE2Ck). Actually, it is really easy.

2. Another useful image-editing tool is pixlr.com (http://apps.pixlr.com/editor). This tool is so advanced that you can work in layers, replace color, transform objects and much more. Moreover, you can download it as an app for your smartphone and use it straight away. Worth a try!

3. Canva (http://www.canva.com) is also a great tool for creating beautiful images. It offers interesting backgrounds, effects, and also a gallery of various pictures and templates, which can be used to create your own design. This tool is not completely free, though. If you use their templates, then you will be charged 1$ when your projects are ready to be published. However, it might be worth it. You can also use it on your smartphone.

4. BeFunky (https://www.befunky.com) is image-editing tool that will help you to make fully customized graphic

designs, add interesting effects, create great collages and flawless selfies. You can use their templates or do everything from scratch. Download their app for your smartphone, too.

5. Easil (https://easil.com), like Canva , is a drag-and-drop design tool that helps you create professionally-looking visuals for web and social media. Use it to create social media posts and stories, promotions, flyers poster, letterheads and even GIFs and infographics. They have many customizable templates for every taste.

6. Install Adobe Photoshop Express App (https://www.photoshop.com/products/photoshopexpress) and you will get some Photoshop functionality on your smartphone for free. You will be able to crop, straighten, rotate, flip, color, remove red-eye and use such filters like Vibrant, Superpunch, and Glow. Plus, you can add borders and frames to the photos. A quick solution for editing pictures on your smartphone.

7. One more great app for your smartphone is Snapseed. It is available for both Android and Apple users. Thanks to this app, you will be able to edit photos on your smartphone. It provides multiple effects and filters so that you can

enhance your photos and make them more expressive and eye-catching.

8. Create images faster & easier with Stencil (https://getstencil.com). It offers templates with optimal sizes for social posts, ads, and custom sizes for your blog images. Create, preview and share them on social media as though they're live. Also use Stencil's Internet browser extension (Chrome/Firefox/Safari) to add text to any picture that you found online.

9. Snappa (https://snappa.com) – a powerful and easy to use tool. Drag and drop your design elements to create eye-catching images in minutes. Add effects and import your own custom fonts. Enjoy their photo library and use beautiful templates. Worth a try.

Image creation for social media may really be time-consuming. Especially considering the fact that various image sizes are needed for every single post if you are going to publish it on multiple social media platforms. For example, if you want to post your sales promotion visual on Twitter, Facebook and Pinterest, you will need to create it in three different sizes in order to adjust them to the requirements of each platform. If you also want to post it on your web page or blog, then you will need one more custom size.

This is when the tool Landscape (https://sproutsocial.com/landscape) can be handy. Simply upload your image and select all the social media platforms and sizes you need this image to be cropped to (covers, profile pictures, newsfeed, etc.). The tool will do the job for you and will crop your image to all the necessary sizes in seconds. You will only need to download them to your computer and add texts if necessary. Social Image Resizer (https://bit.ly/2pm5auy) is a similar tool. Use the one you like better.

As you can see, there are many online tools that you can use for image creation and photo editing. And you don't have to be a professional designer to do that. There are even more free tools that you can use for creating your social media posts, logos, banners, GIFs, videos and other visuals. Since this is not the scope of this book, I won't cover them here but you can get an exhaustive list of them in my book "**100+ Free Tools to Create Visuals for Web & Social Media**" to have a full list of the free resources and tools.

If you would like to learn more about the main principles of composition, color theory, and typeface usage to create really good looking designs check out my book **The Visual Design Principles for Advertisers & Marketers**. After reading it, you will be able to avoid amateurish mistakes and your designs will become more effective and attractive.

## Tools for Video Content Creation

Did you know that 53% of people want to see more video content from marketers? Or that 51.9% of marketing professionals worldwide name video as the type of content with the best ROI? This shows how important video content is for achieving your marketing goals. So, let's look at the tools you can use for creating and sharing your video content effectively.

If you have recorded a video – either while having fun with your cat or during a serious business conference, you might want to adjust its size for posting on different social media. Maybe you need to make your video square for your Facebook profile or trim it to vertical (portrait mode) for your Instagram stories. In this case, Crop and Trim video app (https://bit.ly/2XLEJgN) will help. It will crop your video to any social media or other custom size you need. Here is an equivalent app for iPhone users: https://apple.co/2C9YIMM.

Moreover, you don't need to send your video from smartphone to your computer to do editing, because you can edit it directly on your phone with PowerDirector Video Editor App (https://bit.ly/1Fas1a4). It provides powerful multiple track timeline video editing with free video effects, slow motion, reverse video, background editing and many other features. Edit your video and share it on social media straight away. Similar apps for are Kinemaster (https://www.kinemaster.com) and Quik (https://quik.gopro.com/en).

1. Once you have created your video, you will need to distribute it across your social media profiles. You can do it manually and upload your video to each channel separately or upload your video to multiple channels (YouTube, Vimeo, Facebook and others) at once with a cool app Vid Octopus (https://vidoctopus.com).

2. Do you have a YouTube channel? Then most probably you need a cool intro video for it. Don't be afraid. You don't need to be a professional video editor to create one. Use this free app – Video Intro Maker with Music (https://bit.ly/2ArDSdy). It offers great visual effects and music to create your YouTube intro or simple and short social media video posts.

3. Similar online tools are Render Forest (https://www.renderforest.com) and Adobe Spark (https://spark.adobe.com/make/video-intro-maker). They have free and paid plans. So, you can choose what works best for you.

4. When your video and its intro are ready, you will need an eye-catching thumbnail. No, you don't need to hire a designer to make one. Use this free tool https://www.picmaker.com for creating YouTube video thumbnails. Or, enjoy the cool features of Adobe Spark (https://spark.adobe.com/make/youtube-thumbnail-maker), Canva (https://www.canva.com/create/youtube-thumbnails) or FotoJet (https://www.fotojet.com).

5. The last step is adding a professionally looking outro to your video. It will help direct your audience to your other YouTube videos. Now, online tools like Outro Maker (https://outromaker.com) and Tube Arsenal (https://tubearsenal.com/free-outro-maker) may be handy. Although they are not free, the prices are small enough for the quality.

6. You can almost fully automate your video content creation with Lumen5 (https://lumen5.com). This tool is powered by artificial intelligence and will generate automated videos from your existing blog posts. Simply enter a link to an article or blog post and Lumen5 will automatically fetch the content and populate your storyboard. Worth a try.

7. If you need a video to create ads and promotions, promote seasonal sales, and create how-to guides, try Animoto

(https://animoto.com). It is an easy drag and drop video editor that will help you to create marketing videos for social media platforms. You will have an option to select one of their many templates and adapt it for your needs or start from the scratch. Free for 14 days.

8.  To create an animated video with cartoon characters for your business presentation, tutorial or other project, use Animaker (http://www.animaker.com). It offers the largest collection of animated characters, infographics, BGs, icons, charts and maps in the world. Free to try.

9.  You can also test the power of artificial intelligence and try Magisto (https://www.magisto.com). It is a video marketing platform that is completely powered by A.I. Just upload your videos and photos, choose a soundtrack from their library and an editing style, and the tool will create a video for you. The price starts from 4.99$ a month.

10. A ton of video templates you will find in Render Forest (https://www.renderforest.com). There is a wide variety of promotional videos, intros and logos, slideshows and presentations, music visualizations and many other templates. Simply choose the one you like, make your edits and publish. Free to try.

11. A useful free online tool for editing videos is Ezgif (https://ezgif.com). It will convert your video to GIF, rotate, resize, cut it or will change its speed, as well as do other functions.

## Audio Content

1.  Do you own a podcast or stream live videos often? Then check out Repurpose.io (http://repurpose.io). This online tool will automatically send copies of your latest live broadcast or podcast episode to your YouTube channel. Moreover, they will be converted to engaging videos and uploaded to YouTube and Facebook, making your content more discoverable.

2.  If you often organize interviews for your podcasts, then Ringr (https://www.ringr.com) may help to ensure a good quality sound. Either you are in the same room or in different countries, this tool will provide excellent sound quality. You can try it for free.

3.  But if you want to receive voice messages from your audience directly on your website, check out SpeakPipe (https://www.speakpipe.com). This tool will help you to increase interaction with your audience by allowing your customers to leave feedback, ask questions and receive your answers via voicemail. You can also ask your listeners to submit questions to answer them during your podcast.

4.  Do you need a script to remember your texts while going live? Then BIGVU's (https://bigvu.tv) reporter app might

be helpful. You can copy and paste your script into the app and it'll scroll down the screen (at the speed you want) while you are talking. This app also adds automatic subtitles to your video. It can be a huge time saver.

5.  If you need to transcribe your videos, try Temi (https://www.temi.com). Upload your file and their speech recognition software will deliver its transcript within about 5 minutes. It will save you a ton of time. You won't need to transcribe your audios yourself or hire somebody to do that. The cost is only 0.10$ per minute. However, since it's not human, you will want to make sure that the texts are correct. This is when one of the grammar checking tools I have listed in one of the next chapters will be helpful. Paste the texts in one of them to spot the mistakes.

6.  A similar tool is REV (https://www.rev.com). It offers transcription, captions and translations of your audios or videos. According to them, they don't use software for transcribing videos. Their team does it instead. Therefore, you can expect a better quality.

7.  You can use Google Voice Typing, too, to transcribe your podcast or video. Just open a Google Docs document, click Tools > Voice Typing. Now click the microphone and play back your audio. Google Voice Typing will transcribe it.

When finished, make corrections if necessary. The good thing about the scripts is that you can use them to create subtitles for your video or as a base for your blog posts. Simply convert your script into an article, make corrections if necessary (add links, pictures and other visuals) and publish. Therefore, you will have a new content and additional opportunity to reach new audience.

8. There are several options for adding subtitles to your video. If you publish it on YouTube, YouTube will do it for you either automatically (maybe a lot of errors) or you can upload your script and synchronize it with your video. If you don't want to upload your video on YouTube but still need subtitles, use one of these online tools: Ezgif (https://ezgif.com/video-subtitles) or Kapwing (https://www.kapwing.com/subtitles). They will do that for you.

9. A very useful and free tool that almost every podcaster or video/audio maker knows is Audacity (http://www.audacityteam.org). It is open-source audio editing software that runs on Windows, Macs and Linux systems. You can use it for recording your audios or for audio editing. This software will help you edit your audios, cut out the unnecessary parts, remove background noises

and add sound effects. So, if you are a beginner, you definitely need to check it out. There are a ton of video tutorials on YouTube on how to use Audacity.

There are even more free tools that you can use for creating your social media posts, logos, banners, videos and other visuals. Get the full list of them in my book "**100+ Free Tools to Create Visuals for Web & Social Media**".

# Repurposed content

You don't always need to generate new content. Sometimes you can repurpose your existing content and present it to your audience in a different way. This way, you can give a new life to your old content, reach new audience through different channels and increase your web traffic. Simply think upon new ways in which you can re-present it. This strategy will help you to create more content in less time. This is also your opportunity to deliver the same message in different ways to analyze which of the ways worked the best.

9 Ideas for Repurposing Your Content

1. Use new stats, quotes, or interesting information bites from your article to showcase something "new" in each social media post. In other words, 5 key findings or quotes in your article could transform into 5 new tweets.
2. Simple re-post the existing content and social media posts, as long as the content is still relevant. Just don't overdo it.
3. If your content has a lot of data, convert it into an infographic and present it again. Make a PowerPoint presentation out of it and use Slideshare

(https://www.slideshare.net) to upload and share it with your audience. Great tools for creating infographics are Piktochart (http://piktochart.com), Visual.ly (http://visual.ly) and Infogram (https://infogr.am).

4. Create a short video with the same or similar content and practical examples. You can publish it on Youtube and then share your link on social media.

5. Try content management tool missinglettr.com (https://missinglettr.com) that will literarily reuse content for you.

6. Use Click to Tweet (https://clicktotweet.com) tool on your website. With the help of this tool, it will be very easy to share texts from your articles as tweets.

7. Record your screen with Screencast-o-matic (https://screencast-o-matic.com) or Loom (https://www.useloom.com) to create tutorials. Or, organize webinars with GoToWebinar (https://www.gotomeeting.com) or Eventbrite (https://www.eventbrite.com) to list your webinar and manage the signups. Choose topics you have covered in your blog posts, create videos and publish them on YouTube to drive additional traffic to your website.

8. Turn your old blog posts into guides or eBooks. If you have

blogged a lot about a specific topic, repack those blog posts into a useful guide. You can do this either manually or use BlogBooker (https://www.blogbooker.com) that will turn your blog posts into an ebook.

9. If you find questions about topics you have covered in your blog posts on Quora, answer them and include links to your more in-depth blog post answer.

However, only repurpose evergreen content. It's not a good idea to repurpose blog post with an outdated data. The information must be valuable and relevant over the months or even years. Anyway, cross- promoting your content across multiple channels is a great way to make sure that your audience gets the content they want in the format they prefer.

## Curated Content

Content curation involves finding good quality content that's been created by other people, summarizing and sharing it. Curation is a win-win-win strategy: you need content to share; websites and blogs need more traffic; and people need useful information to read.

Creating a stream of social media content is time and energy consuming. Therefore, begin by setting aside a few minutes every day or week to collect articles and posts regarding your topic. Devote ten minutes at the start of your workday, throughout lunch or at the end of the day. The more it's a habit, the simpler it'll be. You need to compile a weekly list of the most informative and interesting pieces of content to share to your audience. Employ a content curation tool to make the process easier.

The simplest way to find content is to use the features that are already built-in in your social media platform. I already discussed them in the chapter about spying on your competitors. You can use the same features also for monitoring influencers in your niche.

1. A good idea also is to monitor blog posts produced by other players in your niche. Feedly (https://feedly.com) can help you to do that. It is a RSS reader, which pulls in articles from multiple blogs in a curated list automatically. You decide on topics you would like to follow and add blogs that post articles on these topics. Feedly will do the rest.

2. If you want to monitor multiple blog feeds (including your own) and work with several social media accounts, use DrumUp (https://drumup.io). It will save your time by letting you manage and share content in a single place. It also provides hashtag recommendations and social analytics.

3. You can also promote your blog posts or curated content across all your social media channels with Dlvr.it. All you need to do is specify the source where you want to pick the content up from and the platform where you want to put it. Therefore, you won't have to set up a tweet, Facebook post, LinkedIn update, etc. and will save your time.

4. Use Scoop.It (https://www.scoop.it) or Paper.li (http://paper.li) to turn content from other resources into a digital newspaper. These tools will find relevant and

shareable content according to your keywords and turn it into a newsletter that you can send to your audience. Or, use this list for posting on your social media profiles. Both tools offer free and paid plans.

5. To automatically pull together content from the web according to your keywords, use YourVersion (http://www.yourversion.com). It can help you discover good content. You can view the gathered content on the site or get an email digest with the latest updates. Additionally, you can bookmark that content for later or share it on social media.

6. More advanced content curation tools are PublishThis (https://www.publishthis.com) and ContentGems (https://contentgems.com). They automatically curate high-quality content from various sources so you can share it on social media, via e-mail or on your website. The content can be found by searching for keywords, topics and places. These apps work like a single destination for anyone at your company to see what is going on in your niche.

7. Find trending content with a content curation tool, Content Studio (https://contentstudio.io). It will help you find articles, videos, images, GIFs and quotes – in any

industry or niche. Therefore, you will be able to use the momentum to attract more readers.

8. Or, try UpContent (https://www.upcontent.com). This tool will find the most relevant results according to your topic and filter them by influence or shareability. Therefore, you will be able to choose and schedule the best content for sharing on social media. It is free for a single user with a single topic.

9. Get additional benefit from sharing curated content by adding a custom call-to-action (CTA) to every link that you share to your audience. Each time somebody opens the link you have created with Snip.ly (http://snip.ly), he will see your CTA on the bottom of the opened page. Therefore, you will be able to link back to your site and build your email list. It doesn't matter who owns the content. You can add your CTA to any piece of content you share anywhere. Additionally, Snip.ly will provide you with analytics so that you know which content works best. In the example below, I have added my CTA to the blog post written by digital marketing influencer Nail Patel.

10. Use BuzzSumo (http://buzzsumo.com) to find the most shared content topic-by-topic and influencers. This is a rather expensive service; however, you can get some features for free. Just write your keywords in their search tab and BuzzSumo will show you the top content with your chosen keywords that is shared the most across multiple social media platforms. This will give you an idea on what the trends are and what topics people in your niche are interested in. Filter the results by date, language, country, content type and other parameters. If you use their free trial or paid services, you will also be able to see backlinks and shares of each article.

11. Social Bakers Suite (https://www.socialbakers.com/suite) provides similar functionality. Get either their free or paid plan and check out "Inspiration" section. You will find a list of highly shared content according to your keywords. This is where you can get inspiration for your own content or share the content created by others.

12. If you are looking for cool videos to share on your social media profiles, check out Vidinterest (https://vidinterest.tv). This content curation tool focuses specifically on video content and collects content from YouTube, Vimeo and DailyMotion. You can filter videos by popularity and see what's currently trending.

13. Do you want to save and organize video playlists? Then Huzzazz (https://huzzaz.com) may be handy. It will help you discover popular videos on YouTube and Vimeo so that you can use them for inspiration, share on social media or your website.

# Check Your Texts for Style and Grammar Mistakes

As marketers, we write a lot — social media posts, blog posts, sales pitches, conversations with followers, press releases and more. I have listed some apps below that check for spelling, grammatical, and punctuation errors as we type. These apps will warrant that your writing is free from mistakes.

1. If you need a tool that ensures that your email messages, documents, and social media posts are clear and error-free, use Grammarly (https://www.grammarly.com). It will scan your texts for common and complex grammatical mistakes and suggest how to correct them. Grammarly works on various websites, Gmail and social media platforms like Facebook, Twitter, Linkedin, and others. It also works on smartphones. Unfortunately, it currently supports only English language.

2. LanguageTool (https://languagetool.org)- checks your texts for style and grammar problems everywhere on the web. This tool recognizes even errors like mixing up there/their, a/an, or repeating a word, and it can detect some grammar problems, too. It supports more than 25

languages, including English, Spanish, French, German, Polish, and Russian.

3. Sometimes while writing a post for social media or blog, you may need ideas for synonyms to avoid repeating the same words. In this case, a Google Chrome extension, Power Thesaurus (https://www.powerthesaurus.org) may be extremely helpful. Simply click on the button in your toolbar and find all synonyms and antonyms you need. Or, select any word on a web page and right-click on it to see the variations.

# Translate Texts Quickly

Whether it's for business, marketing, travel or other interest, being able to quickly translate texts from different languages is really helpful. The tools listed below will make translating fast and easy both: on your computer and smartphone.

1. ImTranslator (http://about.imtranslator.net) – add this extension to your browser toolbar and get your texts translated quickly without leaving your page. Simply click on their icon, and a small window will open. You can either write your text in their tool or select it on the webpage you are visiting, and it will be translated to your preferred language. Moreover, you can use their dictionary to translate.

2. Google Translate Extension – translate the whole webpage you are visiting with one click of your mouse. Or, translate just separate words. Simply click on the app icon whenever you need it. Additionally, use Google Translate app (Android or iOS) on your smartphone. You will be able to translate between 103 languages by typing, use camera to translate text instantly and do two-way instant speech translation.

3. Microsoft Translator (https://translator.microsoft.com) is a similar app you can use for translating written texts and texts into photos and screenshots. Moreover, you can use this tool to translate speech and use its split-screen mode for two participants having a bilingual conversation. It's an interesting tool to play with.

# Post at the Best Times to Engage

First, you need to plan how often you will share content. Therefore, look at the suggested posting frequency for each specific social network. These suggestions are based on 14 social media frequency studies summarized by CoSchedule.

- Facebook: 1 post a day, curate one every other day
- Twitter: 15 tweets a day, curate seven tweets per day
- LinkedIn: 1 post a day, curate one every other day
- Pinterest: 11 Pins a day, Repin at least five Pins per day
- Google+: 2 posts a day, curate one every other day
- Instagram: 1–2 posts a day, curate one a day

The shorter the news feeds cycle is, the more often you need to post. For example, the average lifespan of a tweet is about 18 minutes. This is why you need to tweet at least 15 times a day to reach a bigger share of your audience. Other social media platforms have different posting lifetimes. You can typically expect that your Facebook post will last for five to six hours, but Instagram post – for up to 48 hours. Therefore, the daily posting frequency differs on all platforms. As you can see, you need to create and curate a lot of content to be able to keep up with the posting frequency required.

If you asked three social-media "experts" a question "what is the best time to post on each platform?", you'd get five different answers. Therefore, my advice is to test what posting times work best for you and your followers. First, post your content on social media at random times and days, analyze the results and see which posting times worked the best. Don't just blindly follow the common generalizations such as "Share on Facebook on the weekend" or "Share on Twitter in the evening." Your followers' activity may differ very much because of their age and occupation. If they work in the entertainment business and are very busy on weekends, most probably they will consume content in different times than if your followers are office workers.

The easiest way to evaluate your followers' activity on each social media platform is to check out the Insights or Analytics the platform provides. For example, there is "Posts" section in Facebook Insights where you can see statistics on when and how many of your fans are online on a particular day and time. You can find similar statistics in Twitter analytics and Instagram insights.

However, there are also other tools you can use for finding the best posting times.

1. Use Followerwonk (https://moz.com/followerwonk) for Twitter. Sign up and generate a report of your Twitter followers. When it's ready, open it and scroll down to the graphic of most active hours of your followers. There, you will find a button that allows you to integrate scheduling optimization with Buffer. Just state how many times a day you'd like to tweet, and Followerwonk will create a schedule for you based on the top hours your followers are most active.

2. One more tool for analyzing the best times for tweeting is Tweriod (https://www.tweriod.com). It will analyze the last 1000 of your followers and their tweeting activity and give you free suggestions on what times to tweet to get the most exposure.

However, there are also many post scheduling tools that automatically calculate the best time to post on each social media platform. Let's look at them in the next chapter.

Post Scheduling and Social Media Management

If you have a life outside social media, you probably can't manually share posts throughout the day across multiple social media platforms. Twitter alone can completely kill your personal life, considering that you need to post 15 times a day, which is approximately once every hour. But if you manage multiple social media accounts for multiple brands, there is no way you could do that manually. Using tools to schedule and distribute posts is a normal practice. Moreover, it is a smart way to be more productive. However, you can mix scheduling and automation with real-time posting to make communication more personal.

So, I have created a table **with free functionality comparison** of most popular scheduling tools. It will save your time on trying to figure out which tool would suit your needs best. However, keep in mind that I have compared only their free plans. If you choose a paid plan, you will get much broader functionality.

| Feature | Friends + Me | Buffer | Hoots uite | Every post | Crowd fire | Later | CoSch edule | Dlvr.it |
|---|---|---|---|---|---|---|---|---|
| Social Media Accounts | 2 | 3 | 3 | 1 | 1 per social media | 1 | 1 | 1 |
| Scheduled Posts per Social Account | 5 | 10 | 30 | 10 | 10 | 30-50 | 15 | 10 |
| *Supported social networks* | | | | | | | | |
| Google+ | yes | yes | | | | | yes | yes |
| Facebook | yes | yes | yes | yes | yes | yes | yes | yes |
| Linkedin | yes | yes | yes | yes | yes | | yes | yes |
| Twitter | yes | yes | yes | yes | yes | yes | yes | yes |
| Tumblr | yes | | yes | yes | | | yes | yes |
| Pinterest | | | yes | | | yes | yes | yes |
| Instagram | | yes | yes | | yes | yes | | yes |
| | | | | | | | | |
| Link Shortening | yes | yes | yes | yes | yes | | | yes |
| Content Curation | | | yes | yes | yes | yes | yes | yes |
| Best Time to Post | | | | | yes | | yes | yes |
| | | | | | | | | |
| Browser Extension | yes | yes | yes | | yes | yes | yes | yes |

| Mobile App | yes | yes | yes |  | yes | yes | yes |  |
|---|---|---|---|---|---|---|---|---|
| *Paid plan starts from* | 7.50$ | 15$ | 29$ | 9.99$ | 7.48$ | 9$ | 60$ | 8.29$ |

There are few more post scheduling tools that are worth mentioning in this book. They focus only on one or two social media platforms; however, if you don't need other platforms, then they could be a good solution for you.

PostPlanner (http://www.postplanner.com) – is a popular tool for Facebook and Twitter post scheduling. Their paid plan starts from 3$/month (billed annually). In my opinion, the best feature of PostPlanner is the ability to find popular content so you can share it with your audience. They use a 5-star rating system to evaluate the content by popularity. Content with the most likes, comments, shares, retweets, etc. get the highest ratings. Therefore, you can always choose the most engaging content to share with your audience.

If you need a social media management tool for Twitter only, then TweetDeck (https://tweetdeck.twitter.com) can be all you need. It's absolutely free and offers a wide range of functionality. You will be able to not only schedule tweets, but also monitor mentions, comments, your Twitter lists, see trending hashtags, new followers and have other functionality. It's a must-have tool for every serious Twitter marketer.

One more free social scheduler tool for Twitter is SocialOomph (https://www.socialoomph.com). It will schedule your tweets and track keywords and mentions. If you also want to use it for other social media platforms like, Facebook, Pinterest and Linkedin, you will need to get their paid plan. It costs 17.97$ for two weeks.

If you focus on Pinterest and Instagram, then you may want to consider Tailwind (https://www.tailwindapp.com). It will schedule posts, help you discover content and monitor conversations. Additionally, it will optimize your Pinterest and Instagram schedules based on when your audience is most engaged. Tailwind also provides insight into your Pinterest and Instagram profiles performance by providing more detailed statistics. Start with their free trial and proceed to their paid plan (9.99$ a month), if it suits you.

Preview (https://thepreviewapp.com) is a smartphone app (Android/iOs) for scheduling Instagram posts that works like a visual planner. It provides you a functionality that helps predict what your feed will look like before you post anything on Instagram. It will also track your performance, offer best times to post and suggest best hashtags. Use it also for curating your Instagram content. They offer basic functionality for free. If you want to unlock their advanced features, it will cost 7.99$/month.

# Automate Your Social Media Listening

It is very important to follow what's going on here to analyze conversations, your competitors and build relationships and partnerships. Monitor what people say about your brand on social media, see what kind of content your followers and competitors publish, answer relevant questions like posts, engage and connect. But it wouldn't be reasonable to spend hours reading different social media posts and trying to find some useful information bits. Therefore, you need to automate everything as much as possible.

**Let's look at 9 ways you can automate your social media listening.**

1.  One of the simplest ways you can monitor important Twitter profiles and their tweets is by creating several Twitter lists. Do it similarly as I showed you in the chapter about competitor analysis. For example, you could create the following lists:
    *   PR list with users (journalists and bloggers) who could help you with public relation articles

- Influencers – to keep up to date with all the current trends and spy on their marketing tactics
- Customers - to see what is important to them
- Competitors – to see what they are doing and what marketing methods they are using on Twitter
- "People to engage" – the essence of all the lists, where only the users you want to regularly and actively engage with in the given period are included. Just spend few minutes a day engaging with the tweets and persons included in this list. Reply to their tweets, like and retweet and build relationships with them.

2. Use Twitter advanced search to conduct your Twitter market analysis: find tweets originating in your locality, track Twitter profile and specific keyword mentions, see interactions between different Twitter accounts, find the right people to follow, keep up with the news and find useful content to read and interesting content ideas. Save your search parameters so that you can easily check the actual results whenever you wish. (At the moment, Advanced Search is only available on the web app).

3. If you want to see the list of everybody who has

mentioned you on Twitter, just go the Twitter Mentions section. Monitor all the mentions here and reply and comment on them, if you wish. It's simple and you don't need any additional tools.

4. TweetDeck (https://tweetdeck.twitter.com) will help you manage multiple streams and monitor keywords, hashtags, your mentions and other activities on Twitter. If you find something interesting, comment, retweet and like it directly on Tweetdeck. You can use it for scheduling your posts, too.

5. Use Warble (https://warble.co) to get email notifications when the topics of your interest are mentioned in tweets. Create your free account to receive emails with the list of all tweets that include your chosen keywords and hashtags. 100% free. It's a great way to be informed what your audience is talking about so that you can respond to them and create conversation.

6. A similar tool is TalkWalker (https://www.talkwalker.com/alerts). Use it to monitor Twitter, news sites, blogs and discussions for interesting new content about your topics, brand, competitors, events or any important topic in different languages. It can be

used as a Google Alerts (https://www.google.com/alerts) alternative or as additional source of information.

7. Use Social Searcher (https://www.social-searcher.com) to monitor mentions on different social media. Just write the handle you want to monitor in their search engine and see the results. You will get a full list with all mentions in your chosen period, the authors of mentions, top keywords, hashtags, sources and other statistics. Free of charge.

8. Set up Google alerts about the topics you are interested in and be up to date on the news in your industry. It's an easy to implement tactic for monitoring the trends in your niche.

9. Use Social Mention (http://socialmention.com) to monitor mentions on different social media. Just write the handle you want to monitor in their search engine and see the results. You will see a full list with all mentions in your chosen period, the authors of mentions, top keywords, hashtags, sources and other statistics. Free of charge.

# Get Inspiration from Competitor Ads

One of the most difficult parts of creating a new ad campaign is choosing the design concept and sales pitch. There are unlimited possibilities, so how to choose the best one? It's a good idea to look at your competitors' ads to get inspiration. Use Moat (https://moat.com) to see the ads that are promoted in Google's Display Network or on social media to get inspiration and new ideas. Simply enter the name of the brand and start browsing their PPC ads. It's free. Note the best examples you have found and ask your designer to use a similar design concept for your ads. However, do not copy it 100% and make sure that your visuals align with your brand guidelines. You can also search for PPC ads of global brands like Schweppes, Adidas, Mercedes and others to get extra inspiration. They hire the best designers so you can be up to date with the current design trends and learn from the best.

Similarly, you can use the free Ad Espresso (https://adespresso.com/ads-examples) tool to see your competitor's ads on Facebook. It is a free tool that provides a huge database of published Facebook Ads. Use this tool to spy on your competitors' content strategy and get inspired by marketing visuals of big brands.

# Save Content Ideas and Organize Tasks

There is so much information on the Internet. It's a good idea to save useful articles, images, videos and quotes that you found on the Internet to use them later. Thanks to the tools I have listed below, you can turn your saved resources into tasks, set reminders, and add notes to plan your social media content. Go through the list and choose your favorite tool.

1.  Pocket (https://getpocket.com) - save the articles, images, videos and other interesting content you found while you were surfing the Internet to check them out later. Simply click on the Pocket button in your bookmark toolbar and your chosen article will go straight to your Pocket. Add tags to organize your content and find it later. Pocket syncs across devices so that later you can find all the information you saved on any of your devices.

2.  Google Keep Chrome Extension (https://www.google.com/keep) – similarly, like with Pocket, you can save articles, images, videos or quotes with this tool to check them out later. You can also add reminders to your saves if you have tasks associated with

them, take notes for additional detail and add labels. This extension can be synced across all the platforms that you use – including web, Android, iOS and Wear. Get it on Google Play.

3. If you want to save links with useful articles to read them later offline, use Instapaper (https://www.instapaper.com). Create your account and Instapaper will sync the articles and videos on all your devices - iPhone, iPad, Android, or Kindle. Therefore, you will be able to read everything you saved on any of your devices, even while you are offline.

4. For those who prefer reading web content on their Kindle devices, Send to Kindle (http://www.klip.me/sendtokindle) may be a great solution. It will push your chosen web content to Kindle so that you can read it on your device.

5. A more advanced tool is Evernote (http://www.evernote.com). It will help you to capture and organize your ideas either on the desktop or your mobile device. Save notes (audio and text), set reminders, upload attachments, or use Evernote Web Clipper to save screenshots and use them later. If you use Evernote app on your smartphone, you will get access to your account from any device.

6. If you don't need multifunctional tool like Evernote and you are looking for a simpler one, check out Todoist (https://todoist.com). It will help you to organize and prioritize your daily tasks. Works on more than 10 platforms.

7. Trello (https://trello.com) - one more tool to stay organized. Add lists, labels, and tasks with deadlines that you can drag and drop. Visualize them with images. You can also set up boards and add cards (tasks) to assign them to different team members.

8. Checker Plus for Google Drive (https://jasonsavard.com/en-GB/Checker-Plus-for-Google-Drive) – if you store your files on Google Drive, this extension will be a good help. Click on its icon in your browser toolbar and you will be able to view, search or delete your files instantly right from the browser button (without waiting for Google Drive's page to open). Moreover, you will get desktop notifications when any of your files/documents are modified or updated by a shared user.

9. You can save a lot of time by recording voice notes. It can be handy if you are in a hurry and cannot write and take notes. Otter (https://otter.ai) is an advanced Android/iOs

app that will record audio and show transcription in real-time. If you want to support your audio with visuals, you can snap photos while recording and use other cool functionality of this app.

# Automate Tasks

I have already listed many tools that can help you organize your social media content and automate posting. In this chapter, though, I would like to tell you about two more tools that you can use for automating other tasks, as well.

Use IFTTT (https://ifttt.com) to automate a broad range of your online activities. From getting notifications for birthday events to posting your YouTube videos on Pinterest, and automatically retweeting on Twitter. IFTTT lets you connect different apps and improves their functionality. If a trigger event happens, the corresponding action takes place automatically according to your settings. For example, if a new tweet is posted, it can be automatically archived in a spreadsheet on your Google drive. You can fully automate it. IFTTT works within a concept of 'recipes' or individual automated tasks. You can choose from more than 4,000 of them. If it's not enough, you can set up your own combination. A similar tool is Zapier (https://www.razorsocial.com/zapier-automation). Except, instead of 'recipes' you set up 'Zaps'.

# Improve Your Teamwork and Communication

Whether your entire team typically works in the same office or you're spread out in different countries, you must still work together to reach a common goal. Working as a remote team can be difficult, although it doesn't have to be. If you have the right tools to use, it can even be a fun and engaging experience.

1. If you have projects that need to be worked on in a team, try Asana (https://asana.com). It will help keep all projects and tasks in one place, assigning various users different jobs as well as set and control deadlines and progress of the work done. It is a convenient tool in case there are several people involved in one project. Therefore, everybody will stay on-task and be organized. Check out also their app for Android and iOs.

2. A cool tool specifically for social media managing teams is Planable (https://planable.io/features). It is designed to be the space for collaboration on all your social media content. You can customize your posts and view them as though they're live in any format: GIF, video, carousel, text or others. The tool offers easy to use content calendar by

vizualizing posts by week or month so that you can see everything at a glance across all your social media profiles. Works as a drag and drop tool to make content creation as easy as possible. Additionally, you can add hashtags, emojis and tags directly on the platform. Since this tool is made for teams, you can share your calendar with your team members and clients so that everyone can contribute.

3. A workspace that can be used for different kind of projects, including social media content creation is Slack (https://slack.com). It will bring all your team's communication together and help to organize it so that you and your team members will be able to access it whenever they want. Everyone will be able to see what everyone else is working on and contribute.

4. If you don't want to invest in complicated tools, Google products are always a good choice. Google Drive (https://www.google.com/drive) (along with Google Docs, Google Spreadsheets and Google Calendar) makes it easy to share and edit files as well as set meetings. Team members can even chat and share notes from within a document.

# Stop Wasting Your Time on Social Media

Although you need to be on social media to manage your profiles and connect with your followers, it can be disturbing. Oftentimes, I find myself on Facebook checking out a friend's post or reading a discussion instead of working on my business profile and creating content. I go to Facebook with the intention to work but end up scrolling through my feeds completely forgotten why I am there. If you are anything like me, the tools I have listed below will help you to reduce the noise made by social media and other time-wasting websites, so you can stay focused on your tasks.

1. Try News Feed Eradicator for Facebook (https://bit.ly/2HrVlUL) to eliminate all distractions by replacing your entire Facebook news feed with an inspiring quote. There will be no distracting cats' photos and videos anymore; however, you will still be able to work on your business page, publish new content and interact with your followers or cooperation partners.

2. If you also want to control Facebook on your phone, check out the app Friendly (http://friendly.io/). It's a light weighted app that allows you to control your news feed

with keyword filters and will sort it by most recent posts. If you don't want to see cat/dog posts, simply set your Keyword Filter to hide posts and articles containing the keywords "cat," "dog," or "kitty". No posts containing those words will appear in your news feed. Conversely, if you want to see more posts featuring the topics you are interested in either personally or for your work, you can set a Keyword Filter to highlight these topics and users. Therefore, you will not need to rely on the Facebook algorithm anymore. Did I mention that this tool will block ads as well?

3. Or, turn your Facebook news feed into a to-do list with Todobook (https://www.producthunt.com/posts/todobook) so that you stop wasting time and start getting things done. Add your daily tasks to the to-do list and see them each time you open your Facebook profile. Just be aware that until you mark them as done, you won't be able to access your Facebook news feed. Or, you will get access to it for just five minutes. Works great if you want to restrict your Facebook usage and the time spent on newsfeed monitoring and reading. This feature is also available on Twitter and YouTube.

4. Our devices and Internet are a huge time savers and time wasters, too. On the one hand, thanks to them, we can accomplish a lot of tasks in a matter of minutes; on the other hand – each app and website is fighting for our attention. They are built to make us engage with them and spend more and more time on their content and features. This results in situations when you sit at your computer with the intention to be productive and work on your business tasks. Instead, you find yourself checking emails, browsing through entertaining websites, watching YouTube videos and reading your Twitter feed. If it's anything like you, get app Freedom (https://freedom.to/stayfocusd). It will restrict the amount of time you are allowed on time-wasting websites. Once the time is up, you will be blocked. You can block or allow entire sites, specific subdomains, specific paths, pages and even in-page content (videos, games, images, forms, etc).

5. If you want to conduct an audit to find out how much time you are actually spending on different apps and websites, try RescueTime (https://www.rescuetime.com). It is a great productivity tool that can be added to both your desktop and your mobile devices. It will track your daily activity to show you how much time you have spent on

different websites, apps and other software. Therefore, you will have a clear picture of what you were actually doing all day... or all week... Maybe, after doing this analysis, you will find a better and more productive way to spend your time.

# Organize your Google Chrome Extensions and Tabs

In the previous chapters, I listed so many Internet browser extensions that if you install at least a part of them to your toolbar, they will be difficult to manage. Plus, so many extensions will slow down your browser. This is why I'll give you two more suggestions.

1. Get a Google Chrome Extension, Extensity (http://sergiokas.github.io/Extensity) to be able to enable or disable your extensions quickly. Just enable the extension when you want to use it and disable when you don't need it. This way, you will keep your browser clean and fast.

2. One more extension you may like is Toby (http://gettoby.com). It will help you to save time on switching between tabs from web apps and websites. If you need to have many tabs opened in your Internet browser, it slows down the computer and creates clutter. Toby eases the process by putting all your links in one window. Moreover, you can organize them, give titles,

create link collections and open several links simultaneously with just one click. So, it's worth to check it out.

# Never Stop Learning

Since you have come to the end of this book, now you should have a starting point for being more productive with social media. As you explore the tools listed in this book, you will find ones that particularly suit your needs and situation. Start using them and create your own social media management system. The goal is to automate processes and save your time and money.

To get the results fast, take everything you learned from this book and put it into action in the real world as fast as possible. In my opinion, this is the best way to do things and develop new skills. Now it's your turn.

I recommend you keep this book as a reference. You may also want to go back through it from time to time.

Thanks for reading. Please leave a review on Amazon so I know what you enjoyed the most about this book and can improve its content if you felt like something was missing. If you want to be notified when I publish new books, please follow me on Amazon.

# About the Author

Anita Nipane is the owner of blog www.digginet.com and author of several marketing books. With a Master's in Business Administration and numerous qualifications in Marketing she has a long experience as a marketing manager and has been responsible for the branding and rebranding of several companies. And yes, a long time ago she graduated art school, too, where she learned most of the design principles that she teaches in her books and online courses. In short, she is the person that unifies marketing and graphic design.

# Other Books by the Author

#1 Bestselling

Free Online Tools Series:

100+ Free Tools to Create Visuals for Web & Social Media

100+ Online Productivity Tools: Get Things Done Quicker

Automate Your Twitter Marketing: Build Your Brand, Get New Followers and Drive Traffic to Your Website

Effective Logo Design: Guidelines for Small Business Owners, Bloggers, and Marketers

The Visual Design Principles for Advertisers & Marketers: Increase Your Marketing Results with Visuals That Sell

Book Cover Design Formula: Create Book Covers That Captivate Readers

Made in United States
North Haven, CT
07 December 2023

45230071R00076